Barman

James Jay

Barman

James Jay

Gorsky Press
Los Angeles • California
2019

Published by
Gorsky Press
P.O. Box 42129
Los Angeles, CA 90042

copyright © 2019 by James Jay
all rights reserved

ISBN 978-1-941576-26-7

for Wilson and Henry

Table of Contents

The Silver Dollar

Finn McCool

The Barman's Box

Around here people approach Literature the same way they approach a Lost & Found at a local pub. They call and call, hoping a person, an authority, will answer the line. *Hello. Hello. I'm so and so. You have a wallet from last Sunday night?* Or, *Did anyone find a blue hoodie, says Lumberjacks on it?* A man, perhaps a barman, will sift through the tattered box, a John Powers Gold Label box that's been made into a makeshift depository for items whose primary commonality is that of being lost, of being found by a stranger, a barman who dropped the thing into this receptacle. The barman looks at what turns up as his hand stirs and stirs about, lifts that, lifts this: only a Catherine Maria Sedgwick stuffed in that corner; just a John Clare babbling about in the sleeves of a Carhartt (Christ, he might be singing); there, a Rene Greig conducting her plays in the dark folds where someone's flask leaked; here, a Bobby Sands huddling in the middle of the mess, the filthy, shivering wretch of him anyways. No, wallets this week. No hoodies, none that are blue anyway.

So what to do with all this stuff? It's lost, always lost, faster than it's ever found. Even a barman, even one such as myself who prides himself in professionalism, in his trade, in helping folks find something of value, a thing lost when good times let your cares wander, a barman wants to redeem last night's late evening, the carelessness of those who came before us. But what to do with this mess, this ever-growing mess? Empty another case of whiskey? Line the open boxes up in the stairwell? Stack them into the second floor? The third? We'll only find shakier, more precarious, ground and more and more obviously problematic metaphors, loaded languages. The English word language comes, in part, from the French word "langue" which means "natural." So this perhaps might be, in part, a natural progression or digression, which is to say a stretch, assuming we can find a tradition, the sides of a box, with which to isolate the new against the certainty of right angles so as to demonstrate its brilliance, its genius, so as to contain them in a way we can comprehend before Happy Hour runs dry.

This might be a problem best left to Saturn, to Kronos, to one who contains time, one who brackets. There are no structuralists lost in this box and likely not in the next yet to be folded one. Levi Strauss left on the flight out of Pulliam last week. And tomorrow, anyways, a man will walk in right off the street and attempt to find a friend only by describing him as: "a terrible guy to talk to— he loves to just paraphrase himself." Fair enough, but we have none; all the customers tomorrow will be quoting themselves directly.

     To which, he replies, "This is problematic."
     Don't I know it, I conclude.

So let's be practical. So much is lost and we look to Literature to find the lost: the intoxicatingly fearful-joy of dancing with those beautiful girls at the Bobcat Junior High gymnasium, the smell of the tulip as the frost melted from its petal, the last words you spoke before you died in your hospital bed.

Practical: *origin: Arizonan, Flagstaff dialect:* Thor, Thor Nolen of Arizona once told my five-year old son, my boy, Wilson, Wilson Jay of Flagstaff while we all worked sanding a table on the back porch in the afternoon sun: *You got to work with what you got, not with what you want.* Wilson, paused, looked up at the ponderosas, inhaled, exhaled, then folded his paper over evenly and began pressing the new grit to the beams.

So what to do with so much lost? Take last month, one of the carpenters doing some remodel work at the pub found a wallet with ID, credit cards, and well over two hundred dollars, U.S. currency. He put it behind the bar by the cash register with a note explaining the find. From the ID, I gathered up a number, gave a dial. Found. While honesty is the norm, the finding becomes the exception. Most of the lost though goes to Goodwill where the problem is passed on to others to sort, to categorize, to discard to still others whom have yet to be born. To those who might yet find.

So here's the rub, the practice of the practical, and what this Barman has gathered over the years: It's okay to find something, if it's okay to lose something. It's as my Marine father said when I was stumped as to what best to buy with my allowance advised me as a child: *You can have it, it's okay to have it; if you don't mind not having it.* The thick syntaxed pages of Sedgwick's novels; Greig's ever severed dialogues; Clare's madcap assonance; they're fine to have, if you can live with them being eventually lost. They will be.

When Bobby Sands composed poems in the H Block cells, he was dying. He spoke poems, lips as close as a kiss, through the cold, metal doors. The sole purpose of those strophes was to sing to his fellow political prisoners down the hallway, to comfort their souls, to bring respite to their tortured bodies. None of those lines planned to survive beyond the long nights onto which they were spoken.

When Bobby Sands died in May of 1981, beaten and starved to death; there was a breath, a pause, a caesura of sorts, onto which other prisoners who yet lived could smuggle his poems out. Later, during a jailbreak, a few more busted up bodies, a few more lines, were freed. In August of 1981 the IRA would print those ragtag verses in a folded and stapled pamphlet. As his fame grew, biographies of his struggles as a peace activist, his fight for freedom also lugged the lyrics along. Naked, wrapped in a blanket, I can't imagine Bobby Sands figuring his poems would last beyond their first speaking. But they did and did. Paradoxically, I cling to them with a hypocrite's fist. They too will squirm from that grasp.

People approach Literature the same way they approach a Lost & Found at a local pub. They call and call, hoping a person, an authority, will answer the line. *Hello. Hello. I'm so and so.* Don't I know it. I am talking to myself again, but I'll press forward a little while longer. Oscar Wilde remarked that his best writing was done during conversation. He too would die from damage done while imprisoned, but to serve him brandies and whiskeys during those crowded cocktail parties, to let a phrase or two or three echo into my ears, their waxy canals, before I returned to the dishes was a delight. So much Literature is lost and never recovered. A great sea of it swells, rises and falls in my soul. On the foam, on the edges of the spirit, it breathes. Surely for every Bobby Sands poem found, one thousand more are lost. We sift, dive, search with what devices we muster. For it's Last Call already. Dinner waits at home, to be rewarmed and I, my friends, must go. Soon there will be no one here. Slainte.

I.

The Slaughterhouse Fly

After Issa

The bees are lost
     in the orange-layered crown
of the poppy
     sprung wildly
in my front lawn—

Bees, fly fully in your frantic
     curves of joy,
for I have no design
     for firing up
the rusting lawn mower.

Like a breeze falling
     down the slopes
of Mount Humphreys,
     may the gods of our
universes tend

to their jobs
gently, if they must at all—

The Lied Lodge

One thousand, one thousand leaves bend on the limbs
of the oak, one thousand leaves like men,
regular old men, sickle shaped, bend to stare at the trunk
of compassion—there's a vacant lot's worth
of rustling in the bar's chatter at closing time,
at last call, thistles of rhetoric blown about and about.

A thin man from Monterrey walks the long hallways
of the Lodge, he checked in under the name: Babe
Ruth. He imagines hitting homeruns while loaded on rye.
The best he does is buy the same named candy bar
in the lonely night time vending machine under dimming,
dimming lights. He clanks his coins into the slot—

There's hope in the company of leaves,
the companionship of the relentless wind.
What pressure to be the trunk who dreams of splitting in two,
so as to find a comrade, another body with whom to speak.
One thousand leaves bend on the limbs, one thousand leaves like men,
regular old men, sickle shaped, bend ever closer to hear.

The Bartender and the Fiddle Player

A man, a musician with a following in the world of Celtic tunes, who lives in the same town as I do (they have to live somewhere too) orders his usual lone pint on his way up Leroux Street on Thursdays. He doesn't say much. Months go by. Starlight piles on the high rafters. Then, mid glass, he locks his eyes onto me. He speaks. His voice like the air in early autumn from a far-flung mountain, meandering through trees and ravines, pressing through the open doorway and into the canals of my double shift working ears. He speaks of the days before his daughter was to be born:

After a prenatal exam with two weeks to the due date, the doctor looked up from her clipboard to tell my wife and me the baby was dead. Nothing could be done, but there'd still need to be a birth. I clinch my right hand on my bar towel. What else could they do? Did he still sing to the full belly at night? Pluck his strings to the hump of terrible news? Did she keep up on vitamin K? Drink herbal teas? Time must have moved as slowly as the Cliffs of Dover dwindling ever down until it was time to jump off the ledge.

Then, the child was born. She was just fine. Fine:
Turns out the monitors were wrong. The data was wrong or something. The doctor was wrong.

I start to ask how. He waves the bottom of his pint at my looming questions. He looks down. His reflection smiles up from the copper bar top:
I don't know anymore than that. I didn't care. It was decades ago and we were just happy to have our little girl back. He adds the *back*, as if she'd always been theirs, already been there, as if she simply needed to find the right notes to follow home.

Stay Awhile

for M.W.

The slaughterhouse fly on the side
of my beer glass in South Omaha has too taken
a rest—*On break or finished for the day?*
I ask his many, many eyes.

You got any jobs for me? He rubs one leg
over his wings, then the next leg
over the same wings. Then?
And then we all settle back down.

Even for a free birthday shot of something
lousy from the well, it's polite, customary
to say please and thank you.
And then we all settle back down.

Samson and the Bees

The first smart bomb was named
Samson. It whipped about a jawbone

until it sat finally down
on a boulder, soaked in the sweat

in the blood in the guts of
three thousand men.

A year before, a test run had been done
on a lion. When the bees built

a nest in the lion's cracked head
they knew mass production came next—

A word, a phrase, as lost now as that stone
upon which Samson found repose;

a word, a phrase given to Samson
by his neighbors. The syllables muted,

it could be translated by select scholars as
        a stupid, stupid lout,
        not a bad boy, but too dull
        to do much of anything—

Arthur Ashe

From Tuba City
the man at the end
of the bar took up

the tennis racket early.
One of the few natives
to do so, he says.

He played some
good matches, and
even met Arthur Ashe.

He's going on
a good bit about it.
He used to play best

on coke in the 70s
just like everyone else.
Except Arthur Ashe.

Arthur. Arthur.
He looks down and shakes
his head slowly at

that youthful past.
Arthur Ashe. Meeting him
is his claim to fame.

A kind, kind man.
The only problem. The sole
dilemma is none of the kids

at the pub know who
he is. "Who is Arthur Ashe?"
the young woman checking out

the pool balls quietly asks,
as if in a library. The barman
responds, in turn, librarian-like

with a shrug.
                    Oh Arthur.
How far the mighty
have fallen. Somewhere there's a golden net

on which your memory matters.
If only you'd leap that divide,
land next to this man

and give him a lift,
a wide palmed pat on his back,
a ride home to the rest of his life.

John Henry

Sinew. Bone. His calves, a pair of diamonds.
His forearms
       flexed like ropes
holding a circus tent down
       during a tornado.
A skull wide
       thick as a slab of stone.

The body as a whole
       constructed in the posture
of No.
       The shoulders,
twin boulders
       that frame an
ever present refrain
       of *fuck you,*
not today. Not today.

Somebody's stubborn, stubborn son.

Mine. Mine.

I am the father of John Henry,
his pa, Jim Sr., who can't see
him like all of you.

For I've seen him dressing as Christ
at Halloween and going
door to door
with mallet and spike
in his ever-strengthening paws.

I've seen his eyes when the neighbors
give him the slow upturn of a stymied smile.
Those eyes so worthy of song,
of praise. Resistance, we all

carry that in the purple marrow
of our bones. Only my son
was cursed with the strength

to smash boulders as if he were a river
rising up the banks. This is what

you all could catch.
You knew he wouldn't stop,
his reason washed out to the sea,
sinking in the mire of a delta
of ideas.

Someone see what I've seen.
Someone give my son
a hand. Someone. Someone.
You—

John Henry's Father

I have lost my son to a tune.
Only a coward would sacrifice
his son for the war machine.

You old men, who look now
more and more like me,
I'm talking to you.

Stand. Stand on the hillside
in the camphorweed and thistle.
If the Huns come today,

better to trip them
with our arthritic limbs
than hide behind

these strong, beautiful boys
that have so much more
to do than bleed

on a rich man's field—
I have lost my son to a tune.
In camphorweed and thistle, I wait.

Sheela-Na-Gigs

His glasses in hand, the doctor supposed:
Well, some women can give birth all on their own,
savage women in desolate lands. It won't,
however, work for women around here.

Throughout Wales, Scotland, England,
Ireland, a thousand years ago, brides placed
in the Christian churches Sheela-na-gigs. High
on the walls, the statues sat as certain as a song's refrain.

With a hangover from the Victorian Era, the Archeologist
early in the morning stumped by a Sheela-na-gig described it:
Repellent, crude, naked female with splayed legs
and fingers holding open a gaping vulva.

With her hands the midwife shows the first-time mother how much
her body will open during birth. In labor the woman begins
to open before the baby even presses the issue.
Her wide-open legs. Her wide-open eyes.

And her curious half smile. Surprised,
the midwife later admits that she wasn't—

On the Main Stage
for Greg Brown

My son calls him Hey Hey.
Uncle Hey Hey in his faded

fishing hat strums a guitar in the corner
of the park. *Hi, hi, Hey Hey,*

my son sings in a whisper to the bugs
shoo shooing on the grass. His song,

his whisper, so many notes soaked
throughout his new mind.

He whispers his reply,
his chorus, to Mr. Brown,

Uncle Hey Hey, like a mason
jar in a field, to Mr. Brown,

Uncle Hey Hey, like a clump
of camphorweed pushing through

an unwalked sidewalk. My son
satiated with voice. Mr. Brown's notes

resonating like nothing else, everything
else resonant in his lyrics as we roll

and rock in song. Mr. Brown, Uncle Hey Hey,
the only reason my boy wears a hat;

Uncle Hey Hey, a guardian against sunburns
for a towhead two-year old; Mr. Brown

the dumb luck protector of the ears,
the bugs shoo shooing on the grass—

Hi, hi, Hey Hey.
Hi, hi Hey Hey.

—Flagstaff, Arizona, June 2012

II.

Pubhouse

"I am a drinker
with writing problems."
- Brendan Behan

Shaving My Head Before the Sun Rise

like Mayakovsky
I tend to imagine
     myself
     as a futurist,
whether I am,
     whether I am not—

Regardless. Regardless.
Unborn grandchildren
sleeping in the wooden cribs of countless
rocking strophes to come,
the muses best love the sounds
yet sung. These tunes await you.

The Bartender at Closing Time IV

Amongst broken pint glasses
      and drying beer
on the laminate floor
      I am

left to my own ambitions,
      over & over
left to my own hopes
      over & over.

It's enough to make a man
      of Reason talk
out loud to Icarus.
      Icarus

Icarus
      over & over—
The sun trapped in the feather
      of a wing

going up & up
      over & over.
Is there no sonnet
      we can hear

from such thin heights?
      Over & over
no melody?
      A thousand suns

waxed,
      over & over,

into wings. One way
       or another

it will come down,
       Icarus,
over & over
       the bleach

hugs the strings
       of the mop.
The bucket
       fills one plop
at a time—

The Retired Corporal in Mexico

for Joe Bibich

Then the waves swell
and he is sucked out to sea.
      Gone.

On our tongues the ocean
deposits dry questions — grey salt
crusted on stones.

An army of memories steps
through our minds, looking
for its lost leader.

On the horizon did he spy an island
littered with giants he had to grapple
one last time?

Or were the wars simply over
for a moment and the current did
what currents do?

Go ask Pablo Neruda.
Go ask Robert Bly.
Ask better poets than myself

for the answers,
for tonight I simply miss
an old mentor, a friend,

and if we're going to do
anything at all about it,
then pull from the pantry the large,

large mugs for Joe's toast.
Tonight, that's all I have to say
       to the sea.

Aloha: The Tank Mechanic Takes a Leave

"My ass would still be locked in Leavenworth,"
he tells me during Happy Hour at the bar.
My Guinness wearing a sip of foam,
I order one more and hunker into

Big Tom's tale of his R&R in Hawaii
six months into his tour
of Vietnam, '68, Tet freshly
passed, won, survived. Marble Mountain melted by a sky

of Puff the Magic Dragons and Big Tom
wrangles seven days out of Da Nang —
What could possibly go wrong?
He lands first in Hawaii with a thick, curled

book of flight schedules, a tome packing
months' worth of flight numbers,
routes, times, all mail ordered for five bucks.
Across the Pacific the mainland.

A court martial. A dishonorable discharge, if caught.
Big Tom's fingers work the pages
with the same confidence they bring to bearings
and oil. He books the red eye to L.A.,

a long layover in Denver, smoke
filled terminals, a lot of vinyl seats
for one more day in Illinois, one more day home —
a day without punji sticks

and tank treads. One more Summer night
in Chicago.

          The riots at the Convention
banging away in the streets

unplanned by the book, and he works
past all of it to see the gal for a few days
who would become his wife and
later his ex-wife, he adds with a laugh

as we order another set of pints;
"My ass would still be in Leavenworth,"
He sips. "If I hadn't caught that cargo flight back."
A bribe of a pilot. Some yelling.

Some shutting the hell up.
What the curled papers didn't account for,
he dashed right into, hunkered on boxes
of rations, the unknown flight

that let him go free, assuming he could live
long enough to get some traction.
Big Tom as quiet as a crate now
dismisses me from Happy Hour.

Our pints on the bar
               like a film's last line of credits—

Black Strap

Old men chewing molasses cookies
and sipping three dollar coffees
at the cafe debate bombs,
gas, gold, and what
the president has courage
to do (or not presumably do).

One remembers MacArthur.
One proclaims these cookies aren't bad.
One talks about greed or something
causing something or another.
So what about the Philippines?
So what? With an aftertaste of black strap,

the conversation continues.
With an after taste of iron, the war.
It's on my tongue.
It's on my tongue.
We say it away.
Say it away.

The Poet at the Apartment Party is Losing It Again

Yes. He's losing it
      again,
repeats the voice
      on the pay phone
from 1962—

You press the hard, black
      plastic receiver
into your ear.
      Are you there?

You are.
      A claustrophobia of beer cans
and whiskey bottles
      pound the vinyl kitchen
counter. The poet's
      debut reading after receiving
a university title or two—

The poet is pounding
      his skull with whiskey
and the door frame,
      babbling about the composition
of sonnets and the nature

of horses and miners.
      Blind to his comrades,
his companions, his
      status, his potential,
he is losing it again—

His mother had arrived
       mid-party to celebrate
the poet's achievement, to
       commandeer the flat
cushioned couch and its
       transient inhabitants.

She finds an ear beside her
       attached to a concerned head.
From the side
       of her frowning mouth,
the mother whispers at it,
       "He should have been
an abortion."

The tone flat, matter of fact
       like a banker or a bookkeeper,
someone who balances ledgers.
       The same voice with which
she drowned the kittens.
       A flour sack,
a brick, a cinched rope,
       and squirming without
a noise as she passed by you
       on Orange Street.

Things were different back then,
       you say
to no one, to the mouth
       piece of nothing.
You repeat that
       it was different,

as if your own judgment convicts
       you, makes you
as guilty as a stone,

as complacent as water.
Are you there?
　　　You press your ear hard,
the pressure sounds like black plastic—
　　　You say as much as a coin
dropped in the dark.

He's losing it
　　　again,
repeats the voice.
　　　Are you there?
In your pocket you reach
　　　for silver. Your fingers
find canvas, dry canvas,
　　　and a past that doesn't care
to be touched.

On Wilshire Boulevard the Veteran
Barman on Break

Jumper's Knee,
they call it.
Patellar tendonitis,
I got it,
but I don't jump nothing
anymore
besides the bar
to bust up a
brawl,
but I know, now,
better than to do that.
And that last punch
between patrons
was thrown years ago—

I'm so slow
in this life
to learn,
and arthritis is faster,
less patient,
than my mind—
my know how,

for however much
that's worth.

I know more of
this life, so replete
with beauty.

I can walk by

cleavage now
without it ever catching my eyes.
The only thing I spy
is drink level and whether or not
to fetch another round.

I can list out three IPAs and make
your choice for you
based on which name I lean.

I can switch you to water,
get you into a cab
before the smell of Naugahyde seats
hits you in the nose.

Like Danny Glover in that movie
that no one on a Friday night
in here has ever heard of:
*I'm getting too old
for this shit.* At least
my ligaments are.
Still, there's Mel Gibson
in the 80s in that same
stupid flick too. His mullet full

enough to cover
a mastodon at La Brea
Tar Pits just off Wilshire
Boulevard.

Smoke coming out
my flared nostrils like
a bad animal that won't
be in the sequel, I return renewed

to duty, to slinging Old Fashions

and Rob Roys and ever

more obsolete cocktails
going down, down, down—

America: Early Morning After the Election

At the diner everyone's
been up late
the night before.

Eyes red, raw,
forcing something neighboring
a smile,

the waiters
do, the best as they
can, their jobs.

The sunlight through
the window is tired, quiet.
The diner packed

in its soft silence.
The adults, heavy cheeks,
sore necks, tight at the top
of their throats,
                    press on.

I adjust my cufflinks,
stand up straight,
button my coat

and step out
to the sidewalk
to listen

for noises
        I don't yet know.

III.

Saturn

"In myths giants are stupid, but they have the maps."
- Robert Bly

In the Kitchen Sink

For the cat-faced
spider I carry on the corner
of my dish washing sponge,

I am the god, the multi-eyed
god for whom he prayed
throughout the dark, dark night.

The latch on the backdoor clicks
open; its sound loud
as a dozen miracles.

Outside when he crawls
to the eggshells atop
the compost pile

it's as if I exist
finally,
as if my whole being, the entirety of my life spun

from his eight-legged need.
And now? And now to do what?
Back up the steps?

On the porch free of all duty,
for all of this, who
do I thank? Who?

Saturn

I imagine you don't think much
of me as a father.
You, in the twenty-first century
and presumably living
in an English-speaking land
where your food comes
in packages wrapped up
as if for a minor king.

I have no hard-fought thoughts
like Athena. I have no leaping
ideas like Hermes. But it doesn't take
much to deduce the likes of you.

So, let's cut the cutesy crap.
I'm not looking for holiday
cards and the most clicks to an electronic thumb.
You're the one who came to me
after all. You told me of your ambition.

Of your home when you
moved out on your own.

Of boards propped up
by cinderblocks lifted
from job sites, the mud
long dried in their pores,
half-ass shelf after shelf
        the thick spines
of books assembled
        like gargoyles
perched upwards by

　　　their sideways names—

Your ambition each day
　　　to crack their checkered hides,

but there's business
　　　to be
done in the business world
on the rubbed concrete
walks to respectability,

　　　so those beasts
wait in glorious silence.
　　　Each of their
lettered bodies
　　　falling into particles
of dust drifting
　　　in the morning's rays of light—

But, as I said, let's cut

the cuteness. I'll be fine after all.

I'll be the one taking care of you.
You'd been better off going to the library,
checking those books out.
Reading them. Returning them.
And getting on with your own business

where you won't think much
of me, father or otherwise—

The Barman's Gossip He's Got on Saturn

When Huey Lewis' "It's Hip to Be Square" launched
up the pop charts, Saturn bought

a hundred albums on opening day
at Tower Records. His thick fingers

pawed at the cash and paid up
in a pile of big bills

making us all yuppies who pay
five bucks now for a cup of coffee
            and more for a pour of beer—

The Poet Versus Saturn: Rematch at the Garden

I read too fast. Always too fast.
That's Saturn for you. Smuggled into your

library. Hidden in the card catalog of obligations.
Tucked into the dry ink of a Dewey Decimal.

In the stacks, pouncing on the chance to check
a task off the to do list. No leisure reading

for you. Your books are overdue.
There'll be fees. Fees. Someone to pay.

Of course we're talking coins, spare
change. Spare it.

Let the dishes snooze in the sink.
Let the clothes crumple in the basket.

Let Saturn tinker with his clocks. This morning
I re read some Don Pablo poems

at the kitchen table touched
with orange light passed through pine trees.

My nose tracks lilacs and lavender
past spondees and turns of the lines—

What Saturn Knows About the Barman

To war with Saturn
        is to find new terms
for fists, for feet
        for spear and sabers—

for Saturn stamps the date
        on every scabbard
on every peace treaty
        like the final word.

All other phrases
        before
become
        squabble—

Go ahead and cut me off.

Arm-barring Saturn

When Saturn has to balance
the checkbook in the tiny back office

for too long as Saturday Night Fever
thumps through the dry wall— He will

eventually devour something. And I'm
not talking blanketed boulders.

Saturn makes a fellow good at chess.
He loves the precision of board games.

Saturn pays the bills on time
until he resents it. You

know he wants to dance some,
maybe lean on the wall and nod

like Matt Guitar Murphy; I'm
not saying he dances well,

but from time to time he wants
to bob to the sounds of something else.

Years pushing a plow; he wasn't afraid of time.
So let Saturn set the schedule.

He's going to do it one way
or another, but you lift the slim, cardboard

time off requests and scrawl his name
on a few; you know he'd never do it for himself.

So Saturn, what do you say?
Saturn, your name sounds delicious,

as if you too are a lover of syllabics,
although you can never say so—

It was Saturn who invented the clock;
who tinkered up the internet;

who put a cell phone in every
American's front pocket.

You big lug, we all know what it costs
to make the trains run on time.

I'm here to chuck stones in a lake,
my hands like hooks. Let's give it a heave.

The Poet Versus Saturn

After hours of verse
on hotel room stationary
    at the Sonesta ES,
it's 8:00 a.m.

As the sun rises
    and fatigue makes a coward
of form,
    Saturn begins to wake,

to take charge,
    once more, of the day.
Where is the column
    you must write for that newspaper?

Surely it must be
    due soon. Soon.
Questions press the sun higher,
    higher into the day,
keeping the sky running
    on time —

The poet becomes
columnist. The poet grows
    invisible as Alpha Centauri
at high noon.

The Businessman Versus Saturn

After years of knocking out P&L reports
and measuring the futility of balance sheets,

I now know music,
music is the best tool

with which to battle Saturn.

His clocks must click
by their measured gears,
making all the seconds the same—

Oh but James Brown bursts
onto the titan's radio station.
Then the red pickup glides

through the merry morning traffic
with the delight of a meteor
knocked into a new orbit.

       Young boys up well
    before dawn from the kitchen's window
        will spy the fiery tail
    passing them by—

IV.

The Silver Dollar

His Voice as Kind as a Foreman Who Mutters
for William Stafford

Lately you write a lot
in your pocket journal.
      Poems?
      Essays?
Don't know.
      Are they good?
      Are they good?
Who cares?

In Hell Billy Stafford and you will be scraped up, bone-bruised,
shoulder to shoulder
shoving heavy lines
into up-down deviled iambs—

In Hell Billy Stafford and you will be forced at dull pitchfork point
to revise
every left alone page
for the devil's polished eye.

In Hell Billy Stafford and you, scraped up
shoving heavy lines
for the devil's ever rejecting rejection stamp:
      the third poem was close, interesting imagery
      please send more material, interesting imagery
      buy a subscription, interesting line breaks

In Hell Billy Stafford and you revising lines,
looking up. Upwards
an old voice,
      shadowed by its echo:
So happy you'll be

                      to not be alone.
You'll hope Billy Stafford feels
you're as dear as a boulder.

Take solace, that's years away.
Push hard and it goes easy,
        says Dublin Owen,
          the weathered angel of the present;
his voice as kind as a foreman
who mutters *you'll do, work starts at 7.*

Say what was that Dublin?
What was that?
Quitting time, you say Dublin?
Push hard and it goes easy. Push hard—
      you'll do
      you'll do

The Dark Art of Corpse Disposal

And being forced to kill somebody in
self-defense is sad, a sad reality
of society today, the artist of disposals claims.

To make it worse there's justice,
the courts, corrupt, incompetent.
First, don't panic, feel like a poet feels,

he advises, as he leans back heavily
into his chair. You've come to the right home.
For love is like a body, repeat

after me: love is like a body,
and when it comes to what matters
most, matters of the heart

as the professionals say, we're all free-lancing.
You have to pick it apart and be poetic.
Don't panic. Being forced to kill love in

self-defense is sad, a sad reality
of society today.
                              How do you get yourself out of this mess?

Act fast for love bloats after a few days, a floater
the cops call it. Love is beset by rigor mortis,
it begins under normal conditions

in the fingers, spreads to the limbs, then rests
in the torso, yet it passes in forty-eight hours, humidity
depending. Then you can again bend it,

even if your muscles, your means
are meek. You can bury it. You can burn it.
You can rent a boat and take it out to sea,

provided you know how to captain a vessel.
It's worse in the winter.
                              And what if the evidence is found?

Well, the artist of disposal says, leaning forward
onto the arm rails, my wisdom
my words of advice are almost

at an end. To you I say best of luck
and don't surrender.
                              Cracked stone steps choked

by thistles and broken glass
lead the way. It's time to take

a step. Don't panic. Bury it.
Burn it. Rent a boat and take it out to sea.

The Dente Sky Harbor Dance

When I'm nervous I use my mouth
to hold onto things.
Books, keys, plane tickets to Omaha,
cellular phones, a sanctioned ID

wear the dents of incisors
as I search and fumble
for the place where I left
an extra hand, a prehensile tail

that swings from a branch
of Certainty, that clasps the trunk
of Understanding. Cave after cave

of unearthed Neanderthals shows rows
of worn teeth in dusty jaws; they used
their mouths like vices, concludes
the paleontologist, while working

on leather hides for boots or who
knows what else. It's a handy
way to explain the erosion,
yet those ancestors never passed

security at Sky Harbor. With so much
on the line, I prepare for flight—

Units of Measure

Saturn counts poems.
Poems written. Poems read.

In designated allotments
of time—

Saturn counts poems.
Syllabics are preferred.

Even quatrains ideal.
The beads of

his abacus glide
like the lips of a stock

broker walking down
a high-rise hallway—

T. Bone Druthers

I know a man named Mister Nolen whose Tibia is Reason, his Femur
is Thought and in his left ankle he gathers the Collected Philosophy
of Eighteenth Century Scotland. "Scots who have," sings the ankle.
"Scots who have." Step by step. Note by note, so Mr. Nolen goes.
Then, one night while stargazing he breaks it all up. It was T. Bone,
T. Bone Druthers who did the job. Or so Mister Nolen would lat-
er say, for T. Bone was big. He did as he pleased. T. Bone Druthers
dug stamps. Wrote postcards. Didn't believe in email. Drank beer
in the shower. Drank beer out of the shower. T. Bone pronounced
the *t h*-es of words as *tees*. From here, he argued, sprang a matrix of
sounds, eroded consonants and shifted vowels that one could work,
by a series of hunches, back to a Proto language that packed sense,
carried purpose, lined out the day like a good foreman or a classical
guitarist. It's a matter of sound and sound.
So crack and crack on the gravel
they go. Mister Nolen, T. Bone Druthers, and up at the stars they
stare. The night crisp. The sky clear. And on Orion's Belt a light, the
second, flickers in the thin air, flickers with something that feels like
the grief of asphalt, like the history of pines. And on the light of
Orion's belt they wait in the road as the cars go. "It's a shame," Mister
Nolen says, "It's the wrong season to see Gemini. And, of course, we
should. We should." And on the gravel, T. Bone Druthers gives his
reply, his repudiation, his thoughts on a cosmos through and *tru* with
thoughts and *tots*.

Last Call for the Silver Dollar Bar

You sit in the pub
drinking 75 cent
glasses of Hamm's.

Behind
the clear plastic
case at the bar's end

there's a stuffed
big horn sheep.
So certain

you are that
it's wrong to frame
this beast

you stew and stare
bottoming out
one thin glass

after the next.
You and a pal,
let's call him Jaba

contemplate the job:
how to steal
this dead thing

and make it free.
Two women come
to the stools next

to you. It's early.
They still envision
something prettier,

so they go and go.
You don't care.
You're almost in tears

over this Big Horn.
Whiskey starts.
You read your Ed Abbey

book. Scrawl in the margins:
"point taken."
"only way to sleep in a tent."

"yes! yes!"
"Carl Sagan is an asshole anyway."
You lose Jaba.

Later, you find out
he got in a fight
on the ice

in the back alley,
KO'd. Nearly froze
behind the dumpster,

but he made it
in time to work
at the hardware store the next morning.

This was your youth.
This was 1993.
You knew Grunge

would change music
as we know it. Place the power
in the people's hands. Certain

of it all. Dad always said
"If you're early, you're on time.
If you're on time, you're late.

If you're late, you're stupid.
Don't be stupid."
You and the stale smell

of whiskey, Mother Love Bone
vibrating your ear canals,
all arrived early. Advice

taken, snatched. You never missed
a day. Certain.
Certain

of the job,
the jobs at hand.
If you've learned anything

now, you're considering
the views of others.
Scanning the Direct TV

for programs, minding
your business.
All that certainty,

the drunk tanks,
the speeding tickets,
what'd they ever

get you? With age comes doubt.
It aches in your knees.
Your tendons scream

with the wisdom of doubt,
so much so that on damp
days you can barely

walk from being wise, hobbled
by wisdom. All that
limping, hiding, reasoning,

what'd they ever
get you?
Curled horns

and a cracked case
shoved in the dusty
basement of the mind.

Put a boot to the door
whispers Jaba.
It's the song

from a best of tape
from a decade that unwound
all over the dashboard.

Now, marketing
turns your years,
your nostalgia into Capital,

while the hits
to the head, the punches
thudded to the time card,

keeps you scared.
So many voices,
the life not so filled

with quiet desperation,
but the life replete
with to-do lists,

transmission fluid flushes,
appreciation/depreciation,
points on your loans,

legislated racism on the news,
collateral damage of the soul,
all those thumps

so when you see the wronged
you don't know
what to do except

get in line, stew on
procedure, creak.
Here comes Jaba, you say?

Lo, here comes Jaba.
Here, to mend Wisdom's
brain damage. Watch

the cells grow
from his two syllable
soul! Is that all

those curled horns
ever carried?
The answer you know

and know, and oh
that's the problem.
Behind the plastic

glass press,
press the bar towel, wipe
and see whatever

thick reflection
finds its way
on a dusty particle of light—

Stylus

The inhalation of his *hello* —
       The goodbye of his *baby*—
hello
       baby
hello
       baby
he speaks these twins
       as if played
from a phonograph
       whose arm
has nowhere better
       to go.

The only weapon,
       the only tool, he wields
against death is language.

hello
       baby
hello
       baby

I bring my infant son to him, to Herman. Here's a fan I tell him,
Herman. He's not amused. He's the great, great grandfather who for
decades has written poems no one reads, or ever will read. For him
the great sea has turned black as a cancer lined stomach. After land-
ing the novels he is aground.

For his part the baby,
       eyes wide and nearsighted,
yields spots, yellowed reasons
       to draw another breath.

hello

> *baby*

The first snow will fall
in November.
> The brown bricks of the ground
> promise certainty, a place to plop
> > a canvas.

hello

> *baby*

hello

> *baby*

Herman has never worried about being forgotten. He's surprised we
already have not. I pull up a chair, son cradled in my arms, and we
talk. We talk about you. You arrive a little late with 2x2s, ten penny
nails, a dozen angles for us to learn. And we do. You, readers of the
future, the only weapon, the only tool, we wield against death is lan-
guage, which you already know.

hello

> *baby*

hello

Private Strophe Stationed in Ars Poetica, America

Sonnets blown about by the wind.
      Sand shaken from worn boots.

American Poetry lives alongside
      the American Military
in the psyche of the today.
So many mouths say poetry is so very important.
So many mouths say the military is so…
      yet no one takes it
seriously—

except for those hunkered
in the trenches,
those who dig like their life
depends on it, which
of course,
it does—

—Rio de Flag, America, 11 January 2015

Patient Groucho in the Waiting Room

Who knows how this mess
of a body works?

Science seems so demure
when the cancer is on your face

by your left eye and the surgeon
runs out the numbers.

Wouldn't a dinosaur femur waved
by your nose better assure your existence?

"Doc," says Patient Groucho.
"It hurts when I do this."

Patient Groucho bends his leg
forth and back, forth and back.

Doc replies: "Well eat this
ginger root, then wrap a hot towel

on everywhere you have a joint.
In two moon cycles you'll be solved."

Which is true. But rest, rest
and rest won't pull your mind's weeds.

If symptoms persist,
reads the label.

If allergic to,
speculates the advice columnist.

Those of us with afflictions
know their life spans.

Those of us who write know
all we have in our narratives

and prompts. When the radio reports
Syrian men indifferent toward

their own soon to be stopped hearts,
beg for help, for the breaths

of children, of women, we feel
somehow Arabic, wronged, and akin

to our lost brothers. Then the cue's struck
for older tragedies to roll

into their leather pockets that round
the arch of the table. Off the rail

we find cancer infects the face
of a poet, so he hires a surgeon

to cut down the ponderosas
in his neighbor's yard. He donates

a case of Scotch to the annual
Rabbie Burns Supper, then busts

his miter saw making a last
book shelf. So many pigeons flap

from lot 89 and a group of vegans
imprisons boulders in ten cages

by a grocery store so that none
of us knows which of the innumerable

the's of each day will precede
the tireless noun called *end*.

John Henry in the High Desert

When in the fourth grade at La Senita Elementary school the boy
first learned of John Henry from the film projector's lone eye punch-
ing its yellow light through the dusty classrooms' darkened air, the
boy kept thinking of breath, of John Henry's breath.

So much power, such force in his swing, how
powerful his breath heaved inwards, belched outwards, so much raw
energy that in the end his lungs collapsed flat as the last note of a bap
pipe left on the floor.

The next day in the school races
the boy slaps his feet faster

and ever fast, a sound like film
at its end slapping the projector wheel in the dark.

Laps on the rectangle field dashed done
in hopes to go hard enough to die.

If in all his speed there was no way
to help his new buddy John Henry—

then his legs of ten years old
would fall still in the last scene.

Separated
from the playground by thin

barbwire the cattle
on the Butler ranch milled,

heads down to the business
of chomping dry grass.

The sun with its indifferent waves
baking the dirt into dust.

Bomb

for A.G.

Bold capitalists a few years ago
wanted to fire
nuclear missiles at the moon,

proclaimed *Time* magazine.
Who knows why?
I say let them.

I don't care what reason they give,
what the glossy pages conclude.
Fire it up.

Better to attack the black eyes
of that cold,
cold face up there.

It can take it, swallow up
all they have, and they always have
more and more.

Better than firing them at
old men playing chess, boards rolled
out on creaking wooden tables in Russia.

Better than vaporizing birds
and babies in Iran.

Better than villages in Korea
blistered to warped, black, glass.

But then someone said they couldn't.

Too silly someone said, an Abbott
or Costello of an administrator

who must have listened
to their reasons, which I'm sure were
bad,
      silly,

           inane—
which is why I didn't
want to know their reasons.

These bombs, these missiles, a testament
to the genius of Newton, and I say Sir Isaac
can get them to the moon.

Hang those missiles up there the way
a hunter mounts elk heads
to gather dust on grand horns

in a vacation cabin he forgets often
to visit—
These bombs have to go

somewhere I figure too—

Fire them up like a boy about to lose
an ear on a bottle rocket filled beach
in Mexico— Fire them up!

Better than blowing up school houses
in Pakistan filled with children
whose eyes mirror those

of my two sons
who read their books on the couch
in my quiet, quiet home.

V.

Finn McCool

Winter Solstice Aubade
for Aly Jay

You say you look old
when I say you look beautiful.

The end of the day hunkers up
heavily in our eyelids.

Let John Donne,
      let August Kleinzahler,

my talented old friends,
write aubades in the morning.

On the back of tomorrow
and its scrawled to-do list

I'll write of love, an array
of diapers, and every dirty dish all done—

I'll write of your Welsh cheek bones,
as gorgeous as a thousand foot steps

      that all end
            at home.

—Flagstaff, Arizona 12 December 2014

On the Dresser

I have a modest tank
for a goldfish who has lived
six years.

He's nothing fancy, a feeder
fish, splotchy white,
designed to be

devoured by bigger,
shinier, stranger teeth.

A half dozen years he's been
the king of his cage;
master of its algae;
the hondo of the gurgle, gurgle
of the pump.

Today, I found out
my wife's pregnant
in this universe so full
of bigger, shinier,
stranger teeth!

Joy and Trepidation
like twin fins glide
my mind through the news.

Raising a feeder fish
into old age
may not make me
a great father, but
in the middle of the night

that gurgle, gurgle
eases my ears —

—Mountainairre, Arizona, 19 January 2010

On the Occasion of His Second Birthday

From the garden,
        across the rain kissed
yard, up the wooden steps &
        through the door
frame, my son carries
        a bouquet of picked lettuce

like an old dog with a scrounged up
        elk bone
like a clean-shaven boxer shouldering
        a championship belt
like a mechanic named Montoya unfolding
        his city issued business license
like Perseus lifting the head of Medusa
        in an 80s flick
like that famed orphan pouring
        his second bowl of soup
like a hobo on
        a ham sandwich
like hand-sanded alligator juniper squaring
        an oil painting

like a boy carrying
        a bouquet of picked lettuce—

Working Up a Sweat

for Pierce Jensen

The feet as fluid as iambs
never cross the twin paths.

The poet works like the boxer works
one   two
one   two
       jab   right cross
           jab   right cross

In the locker room
the boot's laces cinched
with an exhale, an inhale,
then to the square,
then to the stage.

He rises from his desk.
half   step
          half   step

into the blows that knock us
flat out
they go
     they go—

—Winslow, Arizona, 3 November 2013

Finn McCool

My sons bring me the bones,
the plastic frame of a T Rex
plucked from the sand box

where it hid during the fall,
through the winter, the snow,
waiting to ambush the early thaw.

 "Daddy, Daddy," they jointly
chant. "It's the fish." Wilson, the older
lingers on the ish. Henry, the younger

slightly, drops the eff, snapping his ish out
like a line over a wide river. But whose
fish? Wilson hoists the bones to me,

as if I were an old man with busted shutters
and peeled paint on his house. A wreck
of reasoning fiddles with the plastic arcs

of the ribs, until it gives up and goes back
to its spread sheets, leaving us with the fish,
the fish of Finn McCool. "McCool's fish.

I feel it now." Wilson puts his index finger
in his mouth. Henry heaves his eyebrows
up at the sky!

                    The meat and skin
plucked clean, the bones hot in my hand—

A Father's Prayer to Rabbits

Long, blonde, hair uncombed, Wilson works
on flash cards. He sits on the dog bed.
I hold a deck of animals,

and the dog, a dozen years old now,
his black ear flopped over itself, leans in,
like a sleeping coach in a shaded dugout,

on Wilson's leg. Pandas, monkeys, toucans,
bears, skunks, he knocks out the names and receives
his cards, his menagerie, one at a time.

"Make a pile, not a mess," he cautions
to no one in particular. He piles
the won cards precisely.

When we stumble upon two gray rabbits in a sparse field,
he says, "bunnies," a word likely learned in pre-school,
since I'd have taught him rabbits. Some day

he'll say rabbits or hares, or perhaps with a 20 gauge
over his shoulder he'll go off to hunt them,
to kill some fucking rabbits—although I hope not.

If he must, I hope it won't be cruel or a game,
which is itself always cruel in this world
with so many words for rabbits. For now,

my ears say their prayers to these stuck hares
in mid hop with their unwavering tufts of grass. The bones
of my ear canals rub like lucky feet.

Wilson's *bunnies*, his joy as he stresses
its second syllable and leans on its duration, I'll long hear.
The old dog's snore lingers after he's gone.

Bunnies, hold your fading field beyond
the dog-eared edges of your domain,

stay long after this morning's sun walking
the room's wooden floorboards has been discarded.

Overcast

On the black rock jetties, my brother and I crawled
after a breakfast at Hoff's Hut with our dad.
Lichen. Stranded kelp. The taste of syrup still stuck
to our lips. For the tide of ever retreating crabs

we scoured. Waiting for the clouds to burn off.
Time unkind to one and all, to every beast.
All of those skittering crabs are dead
for twenty generations of crabs now.

Sea foam. Shells tossed into sand.
Those crabs like thoughts, like characters
in countless sonnets I'll never write.
Old men stare at dry docked ships.

They sit on benches, sip scalding
coffee slowly, and at night hear
the great fleets moored until
first sunlight summons a glorious retreat—

At Light

My father has no use for flashlights.
No need for new fluorescent bulbs.

His index finger never asked to find a light switch,
for in his sixties he's gone blind. And it's not the dark

that fills his eyeballs. Rather, all he sees is light,
like an inverted game of Marco Polo

where his companions splash waves
of operating room bright white, white light—

In Vietnam a flare exploded in his face,
and the light darted in as a minor character

who would, then, star in the forty years of sequels—
years and years rubbing and blinking back

the rays until the retinas detached dozens
and dozens of times, leaving light,

white, white, light to stay day and night. Enough
to make a man go mad, you might think.

Don't be embarrassed,
I've thought this too, blinking and rubbing my own

baffled and dry ideas of the way things should be.
But my father's eyes have no taste for complaints,

and during the day like Galileo's telescope
he stares square at the sun. His grin mirrors

a lean craftsman palming an oak case, a new lens inside
opening to other orbits. The latch clicks.

The Lost, The Found

Handwritten on paper,
taped to a telephone pole
a lost dog sign posted at zero degrees.
I've walked by its water soaked
paper, its fading contact
numbers for three mornings
now on the way to work.

This morning I can barely
look. The sidewalks' ice
crunches under my feet.
The sign still scrags the pole.
I bundle into my scarf
and trap some of the heat
from my kitchen

                        where my son and I watched
the sunrise. I pulled a chair to the counter.
He crawled up to see out
the window: red, orange, red.
He names out the colors that he knows.
I sip coffee. He sips cider
from a plastic cup.

We watch orange overtake the trees.
"There," he points as the branches take color;
orange, there, there, and there.
It's all over. The kitchen lights off—
the orange now on
our fingers, our knuckles.
There, our forearms, chests and faces—

It's hard to believe this universe
holds us all: boys, lost dogs, cider,
coffee, ice, ice, and compassion—
a thousand cruelties, a thousand compassions,
which I wrap up into this scarf.
The ice on the sidewalks
cracking below my feet.

                Nicky, Wee Won, or Hulkster,
take heed on this January and know
that someone is looking for you. We are all looking
for you, peering into the runny ink
to jot down a number, your name,
in case the same snow crosses our wanderings.
Lost dog, lost dog we're all looking.
                        Find us.

Sharon, Pennsylvania
for Ruth Johnson

And the universe says finite, finite.
The great grandmother reaches for my boy,
nine weeks old, holding tightly

to her bed sheets. His eyes learning sights,
his ears prying open sounds.
And the universe says finite, finite.

She says she will forget this day, this visit,
his surprise, his name, *it goes away so soon.*
My boy, nine weeks old, holding tightly

to her gaze, captures every day, ties
them together in a fist full of songs.
And the universe says finite, finite,

while the furnace blasts the air. The writer,
who I think I am, has no words to summon.
My son, nine weeks old, holding tightly

to his thoughts, morphing concrete and abstract.
His surprise and his name will all go away soon.
And the universe says finite, finite.
My son, nine weeks old, holding tightly.

The Moon's Aubade

While the moon cuts through
the open blinds of the window
over the oak table, splashing its panels,
     I make my notes—

pencil scratches on cardstock.
The dogs snore and snore.
My son in his crib
     in the next room, I came home

to his sleeping. I left
before his waking, while time tangled
like curly blond hair
     in a rat's nest of days.

I consider knocking on his door
to bring him peas and a spoon,
to see how he shovels
     at their elusiveness.

But he is obliged to dream
of dinosaurs, of monkeys, the statue
of a green metal frog. Morning
     brings him the business

of breakfast and swim class. Commitments
bring us so many consonants followed
by the coos of *have toos,* so
     some days we miss and miss.

104

Son, don't ever think I punch the time clock
early for wanting to hear something else.
Don't ever think I fire my truck up
      for wanting to drive away.

Acknowledgments

I am grateful to the editors who first published the following poems.

"After Issa," "In the Kitchen Sink," "The Moon's Aubade," *Curios*, Coconino Community College, Flagstaff, Arizona, 2016

"America: Early Morning After the Election," *FlagLive*, Nov. 17-23, 2016

"Stylus," *Huffington Post*, The Rings Series

"T Bone Druthers," *Fourteen Hills*, San Francisco State

"Winter Solstice," "Stay Awhile," "The Lost, The Found," *The City Inside Me, Vol. 1*, editor, Ky J. Dio

Thank you for the financial support and encouragement from the Friends of the Flagstaff Public Library and its Copper Quill Award, and to Gary Every for the Dylan Thomas Prize.

Thank you to Gillian Ferris and Tim Aydelott, the outstanding poetry editors riding the airwaves at KNAU with the Poetry Friday program and Radio Sunnyside's Words & Notes respectively, where several of these poems were broadcast.

Much gratitude to Nicole Walker and Stacy Murison for their inspiration, encouragement, and fine example. Thank you to my longtime literary partner in letters, Jesse Sensibar, who can haul you out of a poetic rut or deep muddy ditch. Thanks for the correspondences with Mark Gibbons and Thor Nolen, who were first readers of many of these poems and whose replies generated the energy for more to come. Special thanks to Miles Waggener for his long years of friendship and poetic advice and support. There are few things more valuable than old friends.

Thank you to Sean Carswell, the most brilliant and enjoyable editor I can imagine working with. And for their keen attention to detail, insights, and varied perspectives, thank you to the student editors at California State University Channel Islands: Damian Aguilar, Dustin Ariola, Eric Azizkhanian, Ashley Balzer, Leslie Castaneda, Samuel Diaz, Darol Garcia, Sierra Garlinger, Stephanie Guerrero, Ardyss Hawley, Julianne Kuzmanovic, Katie Lech, Eriyana Linder, Mia Lopez, Taylor Lucio, Andres Macias, Jack McTomney, Paisley Meir, Jazzminn Morecraft, Nicholas Rada, Abigail Ramsey, Christopher Tennefos, Madison Traylor, Alma Villanueva, Brian Whalen, and Marcella Wilroy.

And as always, thank you to Aly, Wilson, and Henry, who provide the music.

About the Author

James Jay has worked as a bartender, a wild land firefighter, book seller, surveyor, and furniture mover. He lives in Flagstaff, Arizona where he has taught poetry at the jail, the public schools, Northern Arizona University, and given Irish Literature lectures at Northern Arizona Celtic Festival. He has an MFA from the University of Montana, and for nine years, he wrote the Bartender Wisdom bi-monthly column in *Flag Live*. He owns a bar, Uptown Pubhouse, with his wife, the musician Alyson Jay. They have two sons, Wilson and Henry and two dogs, Emma and Jack (they're a wily pack).

When not writing, working at the bar, and running with the kids and dogs, James Jay plays the ancient Irish game of hurling as a half-forward for the Flagstaff Mountain Hounds. Recently, he received the Copper Quill Award, and his poetry has been featured regularly on National Public Radio's *Poetry Friday* on KNAU.